MANAGING YOUR PRIORITIES AND DEADLINES

Simple steps to prioritise your workload and reach your goals

Written by Florence Schandeler

Translated by Carly Probert

Coaching 50MINUTES.com

HOW TO MANAGE YOUR PRIORITIES AND DEADLINES

- **Problem:** How can I set priorities and get organised in order to make the most of the time I spend at work?
- **Uses:** Knowing how to choose priorities and manage your schedule to complete tasks within the set limits. Never losing sight of your objectives or wasting energy, saying 'I'll never have the time', but planning and taking action.
- **FAQs:**
  - How can I get rid of time-consuming habits?
  - How can I plan the tasks I need to get done?
  - How do I set priorities?
  - How should I organise my schedule?
  - How can I stop procrastinating?
  - How do I delegate successfully?
  - How can I disconnect from work once I've left the office?

With the arrival of the internet and new technology, the rhythm of life seems to get faster and faster. Nowadays, we live in a society where the words "speed", "competition" and "stress" are everywhere. Laptops and smartphones have made us available 24 hours a day. This means that the line between our professional and private lives has become more and more tenuous for both employers and employees, as they cannot avoid their inbox. Doctors have also noted that the number of people suffering from burnout is increasing.

'Time is money'. How many times have we heard this expression, forcing us to speed up and dive headfirst into the pile of folders stacked on our desks? This focus on speed and our hyper-connected world prevent us from maintaining the distance necessary for reflection and questioning of the way we work. Many of us have become accustomed to working under pressure, being conscious of never having enough time, and cursing the days when 24 hours just aren't enough.

Don't wait any longer before reading this book – by investing just 50 minutes of your time, you will be able to reflect on the way you work and how you manage your time. We will present some theoretical models that highlight the pheno-menon of the 'lack of time'" and explain why it is important to change some of your habits in order to emerge victorious. Then we will look at how you can develop an optimal work schedule that will take into account your job priorities and deadlines, so that you can be efficient when you take action.

TIME MANAGEMENT: THE BASICS

ANALYSING THE "I DON'T HAVE TIME" PHENOMENON

Symptoms

> Food for thought: "Those who make the worst use of their time are the first to complain of its brevity." – La Bruyère (1645-1688)

We have all suffered on different levels from a lack of control over time. When we get down to work, we often do not notice the time passing or we run around all day without being able to complete our paperwork.

- We rush our work and feel that we are missing the essential points.
- We accept delegated work from our superiors without being sure if we can finish it.
- We feel like we are wasting time by helping a colleague who is seeking advice and by answering dozens of emails.
- There is still a whole pile of paperwork to get through... but what have we done with our day?
- So, we have no choice but to take the work home to get it done in time.

This realisation drops like a bombshell: we do not have time. Yet, at the risk of stating the obvious, a day will always have 24 hours, eight to ten of which are devoted to professional obligations for many workers. This is a reality that must be acknowledged, so we should learn to understand all its aspects and take advantage of it.

As it would be cynical and counterproductive to imagine the contrary, we should believe that every problem has a solution and put some of our time to good use thinking about it. However, let's start by accepting the premise that in order to flourish and have a balanced life, the key is not working more, but working better, learning to control time instead of becoming a slave to it.

Time-wasting factors

Try to identify the time-consuming elements that distract you from your priorities when you are trying to move forward. We can identify two sources for these: on the one hand, the external factors related to the socio-professional environment in which we operate, and on the other, the internal factors inherent in our individual way of being and behaviour.

Although we may feel that time loss is mostly due to external events outside of our responsibility, by taking stock of the disruptive elements that slow us down, we often observe the opposite. Establish a non-exhaustive list of possible factors.

External factors	Internal factors
Lack of information on the tasks to be completed	Not knowing how to say 'no' to superiors or colleagues when you are already snowed under with work
A full inbox of emails awaiting replies and a telephone that never stops ringing	Being a perfectionist
Unexpected things arising each day	Wanting to do too many things at once, which leads to overworking
	Poor definition of working objectives
	Poor planning of tasks
	Lack of concentration
	Lack of self-discipline, leading to procrastination
	Habit of 'channel hopping' between tasks, which leads to moving from one task to another without actually finishing anything

Priorities and Deadlines © 50MINUTES.com

EXTRA INFORMATION: AVOID THE 'CHANNEL HOPPING' EFFECT

Conditioned by the habits of a fussy and impatient television viewer, in many circumstances we tend to indulge in a form of 'channel hopping', where we continually change tasks or topics without bothering to finish what we started. In the evening, from the comfort of our own couch, it is up to us to make that choice, changing channels because we dislike the program or because we want to avoid watching yet another advertisement. In our professional lives, however, this 'channel hopping' has the consequence of allowing us to accumulate a series of unfinished tasks which snowball and eventually avalanche into a series of imminent deadlines. Here are some resolutions you should make:

- If I start a task, I will finish it;
- When I finish a task, I will organise and file my documents;
- I will sort through my documents and throw away those that don't need to be kept;
- When I receive instruction or I think a task is important to perform, I will make a note of it directly;
- If I have any doubts regarding information or procedures, I will immediately ask;
- As soon as I have finished my work day, I will tidy my desk and prepare the materials needed for the following day.

Although we cannot influence external factors, there is some general advice that you can follow: try to minimise disruption from new technologies as much as possible. When the opportunity arises, log off from your email and turn off your mobile to concentrate entirely on your task, as this will save you valuable time.

Internal factors depend primarily on how we operate. It is up to each of us to identify the things that disrupt our work, in order to make every effort to overcome them. Now, write down the elements that distract you daily. The act of writing them down is essential to allowing the factors to materialise and to finally identifying the cause.

Problems of inaction

Entrenched in our way of working, along with our bad habits, there are mechanisms that make us passive and inefficient. These are problems of inaction. Roger Moyson, an American trainer and consultant, identifies three varieties, with each person being mostly affected by one of the three.

- **Agitation:** This state occurs when our attention tends to be distracted by activities on the sidelines of our focus, sometimes completely unrelated, and this slows our pace of work. People who react in an agitated way towards the activity tend to want to prove to others, but mostly to themselves, that they are good workers. However, running around the task instead of getting on with it is more likely to lead to them not finishing the task on time.
- **Over-adaptation:** This dysfunction occurs when a person wants to please at any cost and does what they think they are being asked to do, without questioning what work actually needs to be accomplished. They adapt their work to better suit what they think the expectations of the boss or client are, losing sight of the intrinsic objective of the task to be performed.
- **Incapacitation:** This problem is more related to people whose emotions easily take over, and tend to respond to their required work and stress with panic attacks, victimisation or anger. Overwhelmed by their emotions, they

are unable to focus on the task at hand.

We cannot totally get rid of these problems that characterise our way of managing work and stress. However, by getting to know ourselves better and being more attentive to the way we react, we can try to outsmart them.

Laws of time management

Some theoretical schemes, developed by scientists, economists and essayists are able to enlighten us a little about time management.

- **Parkinson's Law:** According to this law, work tends to be stretched out over the time allotted to it. The longer we have to complete a job, the longer it will take. An example of this is the work we take home to look at for a few hours over the weekend, and end up spending most of our time on. To avoid this trap, set deadlines. The goal is not to set out in a race against time, but to successfully estimate the time needed for its completion, and to respect the deadline in order to move on afterwards.
- **Urgency law:** This states that when 50% of our working time is spent on tasks that are done urgently, we are less efficient and have a tendency to lose sight of our priorities. We lack the perspective to reflect on our work and our method of organising it. This state, operating in a vicious circle, poses the risk of being ongoing. Scheduling your work is essential to breaking this urgency and stress, where we feel like we are drowning in work, executing task after task without being able to see the end, often leading to exhaustion and burnout.

Laws of time usage

Let's look at how we can manage our working time based on tasks and the way in which we operate.

- **Carlson's Law:** This explains that the brain takes time to mobilise for a complex task. To write a report, correct a first draft or memorise something, we must be totally focused. If we are constantly interrupted by the phone, colleagues, friends, or we are trying to perform another task at the same time, we will not achieve optimum performance or high quality work. Some studies show that after five or six interruptions, we even tend to postpone the task to the indefinite future. To provide faultless work, we must somehow be able to block out the world and devote ourselves entirely to the task.
- **Law of cycles:** This states that every action has a beginning and an end, and in order to reduce working time, it is better to devote ourselves to the task, rather than wanting to undertake dozens of tasks simultaneously. This method provides a more comprehensive view of the actions that need to be taken, and allows us to focus more easily on the end goal. Furthermore, it explains that, according to the characters involved, each person finds it more or less difficult to manage a phase of action. Some struggle to get to work and find themselves procrastinating; others are perfectionists who are unable to complete the task entrusted to them because they endlessly tweak small details. It is important for everyone to take stock of the way they work in order to improve. Depending on the phases of action that cause problems, you can ask yourself several questions:

Before starting	Doing the task	Finishing the action
Do you know what you need to do (description of the task and objective)?	Is your working method effective?	Have you met your objective(s)?
Do you know how to start?	Do you know the final objective of the task?	Are you a perfectionist? Do you tend to do more than necessary?
Do you have all the necessary tools?	Are you governed by limited time restrictions?	Or, do you give the impression of rushing your work?
Are you interested in the task and its objective (motivation)?	Have you completed your schedule (self-discipline)?	...
Have you designated a single folder to concentrate on?	...	

- **Chronobiology:** This takes into account our biological rhythms and invites us to distribute workloads according to them. We have often heard the expressions 'morning person' and 'night owl'. To work efficiently, you must identify which of these you are in order to schedule the tasks that require the most attention for the most suitable times. You can see that a series of factors, internal and external, are taken into account when we think about work and concentration. With regard to the internal factors that are conducive to our biological rhythm, we notice, for example, that the hours immediately following lunch are less favourable for concentration because our body uses more energy to digest. For the external factors, some need a well-lit office in order to feel energised throughout the day, while others prefer a more subdued atmosphere or a source of light focused on the paperwork they are dealing with.

- **Turgot's law:** This law recognises the concept of 'diminishing returns', which explains that over time, after a certain number of hours have been spent focusing on a task, we become less and less efficient. It is therefore important to plan regular breaks and not exceed a certain number of daily working hours. Generally, a ten-minute break every hour is recommended for work that involves a lot of concentration; this helps you to take a step back, while being short enough that you do not become distracted.

CHANGE TO 'SAVE TIME'

Motivation

For any change to be effective and sustainable, you must be motivated. A smoker will not stop smoking if they are not convinced of the benefits they can derive from it. The same applies here. Manage or be managed by your time, the choice is yours! This requires awareness of the 'better-ness' that can come from good time management. Motivation comes from seeing these benefits.

Resistance

By nature, human beings are resistant to change. Often pessimistic, we fear that the situation will worsen, and habits – good and bad – are part of our dogmatic belief that things "are as they are" and must not be otherwise. The perception we have of change makes us stressed and we often prefer to get back to our routine, no matter how time consuming it may be.

For example, some students continue to think that the key to success lies in the spending eight to ten hours stuck in a chair, eyes glued to their work, without asking questions about their working methods. However, if they organised themselves differently, that same amount of working time could get them better results.

To change, we must dare to question and overcome these obstacles, including our fear of the unknown and the urge to return to our reassuring habits.

Objectives

Identifying and focusing on the benefits that we can achieve from better time management is the key to motivating ourselves and succeeding in changing our habits. Among the desired objectives, we can highlight:

- growing personally and professionally through a more balanced distribution of time between work, rest and leisure;
- improving our work efficiency, through a better definition of objectives and priorities;

- completing important tasks on time, through prioritising and planning;
- projecting a more professional image of our work, to ourselves and to others, by better managing deadlines and adapting to the unexpected;
- reduce the pressure of working against the clock.

Defining objectives

To formulate a goal, you must clearly define and describe what you want to achieve. Think in terms of "SMART", a concept attributed to Peter Drucker (1909-2005):

S	Simple	The objective should be described in concrete and precise terms.
M	Measurable	The completion of the tasks needed to achieve the final objective should be measurable, and must give an indication of the path followed or what still needs to be completed.
A	Attainable/ ambitious	To be attainable, the objective should respect all material and human restraints. However, it should also constitute a challenge in order to be motivational. This point is not intended to deter you from shooting for the stars, but setting the bar too low will also lead to a lack of interest.
R	Realistic	The objective should be directly linked to the professional activity undertaken.
T	Timely	The realisation of the entire project must be limited in time by a deadline and intermediate dates that allow you to manage the duration and due date of each task.

Once you have set your goals and tried another planning technique, be sure to evaluate the changes made to ensure that they will contribute to achieving these goals.

> "If one does not know to which port one is sailing, no wind is favourable." – Lucius Annaeus Seneca

PRIORITISING AND PLANNING

Definition

Planning includes a list of tasks to perform, organised according to a schedule: this allows us to manage the allocated time and tends to describe the way in which a given goal can be achieved.

To do this, focus your attention on the goal, list the tasks necessary for its execution and organise them in a schedule that takes into account the deadlines, times and dates of the various tasks.

Setting priorities

- **The concepts of urgency and importance**: to organise your work better, it is important to identify the priority tasks. This notion of 'priority' implies a choice made based on your goals, and allows you to decide which tasks will be done before others. This results from the combination of two criteria: urgency and importance. Urgency is defined by the concept of time, and importance is linked to our professional role and the values of our company.

In order to rank problems in order of priority during the Normandy landings, General Eisenhower established a functional grid by crossing the notions of urgency and importance to obtain a matrix with four entries, defining four types of duty:

UI: urgent and important tasks	uI: not urgent but important tasks
To be done immediately, a top priority.	Tasks that do not need to be done immediately, that can be scheduled for the near future.
Ui: urgent but not important tasks	ui: not urgent and not important tasks
To be done immediately after the urgent and important tasks, or delegated quickly.	Tasks that can potentially be dropped.

This categorisation of tasks allows you to better anticipate their achievement taking into account the time allocated and the urgency with which it is often necessary to work, without losing sight of the concept of importance.

- **The ABC matrix:** To help set your priorities based on these concepts, you can also refer to the ABC matrix, which classes tasks into three categories:
  - A tasks: to achieve according to priority levels ranking A1-A3
  - B tasks: to achieve quickly and which can potentially be delegated;
  - C tasks: "routine" tasks, less urgent and can be done during spare moments during the day or can be delegated easily.

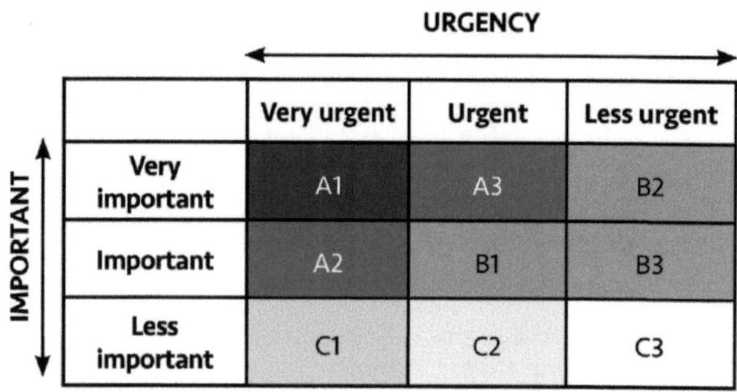

Priorities and Deadlines © 50MINUTES.com

With this matrix, you will be able to list your tasks in order of priority, allowing you to concentrate on the essentials and achieve your goal in the allotted time.

- **The Pareto Principle:** This law provides another indication of the tasks to be performed according to priority, in order to increase the effectiveness of your work. Known in the world of marketing as the 80/20 law (because "20% of customers account for 80% of sales"), it states that 20% of our efforts provide 80% of results, while 80% of the tasks we perform count for only 20%.

Following this logic, some tasks are more profitable than others: question the effectiveness or ineffectiveness of the actions you are carrying out in relation to your goals, and try to eliminate the least profitable, in order to free up time and devote it to a more lucrative task, therefore prioritising your work.

Develop a plan of action

Having reviewed the characteristics of your goal and put the tasks in order of priority, develop a schedule that allows you to take action. To do this, you will need a pencil and paper. Your plan for the day, or even the week, will take into account these five elements:

- **Activities:** Think about listing them. Anything that is not written down is at risk of being forgotten;
- **Priorities:** From this list of activities, highlight those that are urgent and important;
- **Time:** When developing your schedule, do not forget to consider this essential factor. On the one hand, think about estimating the time required for each activity in the most realistic manner possible. Be careful not to underestimate it: never managing to complete set tasks on time is the best way to put you off making a schedule. A little training will be necessary to reach the best estimate of the time factor. On the other hand, in the organisation of your day, remember to consider your bio-logical rhythms: if you know that you have more difficulty concentrating after a meal, try to schedule activities that require less 'alertness' during these hours;
- **The unexpected:** To reduce the stress factor, it is impor-tant to be flexible in your scheduling in order to deal with contingencies. Keeping some free time in your schedule is the best way to overcome this stress;
- **Monitoring:** As with any action undertaken or change made, it is important to make an assessment at the end of the experience. Evaluate the benefits derived from your schedule and investigate areas for improvement in

its implementation.

TOP TIPS

- Advance in the right direction: before wanting to do a good job, make sure you are doing the right job. Having to correct your mistakes is a time-consuming and demoralising activity. A moment's reflection to clearly understand the purpose of the task can save you valuable time.
- Don't lose motivation when you arrive at the office: nothing is more depressing than arriving to a crowded room, sitting at your desk and seeing a dozen Post-It notes stuck to the wall, some of which date back several weeks and have the word "URGENT" written in capital letters. To ensure that your new resolutions don't go flying out of the window the moment you cross the threshold of your office, organise your workspace so that it is pleasant to work in. Only keep the items that will allow you to get to work immediately within reaching distance (computer, notepad, calendar, document folder with recent files, etc.) and think about the comfort of your environment (light, quiet, etc.).
- Focus: you often waste a lot of time anticipating events, stressing, thinking "I will never be able to finish on time". Planning your own work and providing deadlines is the best way to rationalise this fear and not forget anything. To create your schedule, focus on the "here and now", and on the actions to be undertaken and planned in advance when scheduling your tasks. This is partly to gain confidence and also think in terms of actions, by proceeding in stages and ignoring the state of emergency we may face.
- Make progress in the way we work: to make better

choices in terms of your method of work, you have to test other modes and measure results. This assessment is essential and must precede the adoption of effective change: there is no point changing our habits if doing so will be counterproductive.

- Avoid being overwhelmed: to master your time and not become overwhelmed by events, list and concretely plan your tasks in a schedule. Allow time slots for contingencies that are sure to get in your way and force you to abandon your good resolutions. Finally, once the objectives have been clearly established, keep heading towards them, as this implies an element of self-discipline (following schedules, meeting deadlines) and the ability to say "no" to colleagues and superiors, as well as to delegate. This negative response is often difficult to formulate, and should not be seen as a simple refusal, but as a reasoned choice that allows you to fully focus on the current tasks and should be formulated as follows: e.g. "Come back at 3pm and I will have more time for you", or "I do not have time this week to do this. I want to have time to complete another task that I was given and get it done by Friday". This means you won't get lost in a series of secondary, additional tasks that prevent you from carrying out your own priority projects.

FAQS

HOW CAN I GET RID OF TIME CONSUMING HABITS?

We are all subject, more or less strongly, to "time thieves", on which, out of habit or because you believe they are an obligation, you spend precious minutes. Answering the phone that never stops ringing and prevents us from delving into our report, remaining permanently logged into our in-box, or even lacking organisation, which makes us improvise our daily schedule once we arrive at the office.

Here are four steps to help you tackle them!

- Above all, you need to identify them. Note what you think is a source of wasted time at work, which tends to distract you from your main tasks. You will possibly not be able to identify all the main elements at first glance, but by being aware of them, you will succeed in getting rid of them as you go along.
- Once the list is more or less complete, rank them in order of importance.
- Make a list with two columns, one to identify the problems they cause and another to state the benefits that can be derived.
- Answer the following two questions:
  - What obstacles can I overcome?
  - What method should I use to do this?

Once you have established the way forward, focus on the

positive aspects that this change will bring and persevere in your approach. Work through the list point by point, being firm with yourself and making decisions every day that will help you manage your professional life.

HOW CAN I PLAN THE TASKS I NEED TO GET DONE?

When creating your schedule, you have to organise the different tasks you listed previously. Five basic rules will help you in the development of this schedule:

- Organise tasks by priority. The priority of a task depends on the intersection of two characteristics: importance and urgency. Beforehand, note deadlines on your calendar in red ink;
- Mark in your schedule the hours reserved for each task by specifying the start and end time and the goal at the end of each work period. It is not always easy to know how long one task or another will take, especially if you are new to the role, but this planning exercise will make you more effective in the long term;
- It is more motivating and often more productive to tackle only two or three tasks at any one time and complete them, rather than start many jobs at the same time without finishing them. Try to order your schedule in cycles: fully complete one task before starting another;
- Generally, consider your biological rhythm when distributing daily tasks. If you know that you find it more difficult to remain attentive between 1pm and 3pm, don't schedule a job that will require all your concentration for

that time.

- Finally, so that you never feel like you are being forced to work, alternate tasks you do not like with those that motivate you.

HOW DO I SET PRIORITIES?

To do a job, you must have set a goal, knowing where our actions must lead us. For example, if we want to plan a meeting to decide how to implement a new marketing project, one of our priorities will be to establish a specific agenda, which we will make the objective of the meeting. Another priority will be to meet with the interested parties and set a date and a place for the appointment. A secondary task, labelled so because it is less urgent and less important, will then be to provide coffee at the place of the meeting; this can also be easily delegated.

Having defined our goal and listed the tasks to accomplish for its achievement, it is crucial to set the priority of the tasks, depending on the urgency and importance of each. By preparing the coffee without knowing when the meeting will take place or how many people will attend, it will come to only one thing: a waste of time.

HOW SHOULD I ORGANISE MY SCHEDULE?

A schedule is a valuable tool to keep handy. This electronic or paper tool is your entire organisation resource. It allows you to consider your next day's work, as well as reflect on work already done and adopt a critical viewpoint of the way you work and manage time.

Ideally, it consists of different sections:

- A calendar where you note down appointments, deadlines and holidays;
- A "To do list" section, where you register in bulk all of your tasks and deadlines;
- Sheets that allow you to plan weekly and/or daily tasks;
- Extra sheets for recording information that may be helpful, such as addresses and phone numbers;
- A note section for writing down your ideas and experiences. Instead of noting it on a separate sheet, keep part of your schedule for this, so that you can access it easily.

If you make a habit of making your schedule a reference tool, it can quickly become very useful in allowing you to better manage your time and your work, and to note all the important elements so that you don't forget anything.

HOW CAN I STOP PROCRASTINATING?

To fight against procrastination, you should set clear objectives, outlined in terms of the results to be obtained, within a defined period of time. To motivate yourself to keep to your schedule, try to identify the benefits you will achieve by reaching your goals on time: extra time to focus on a file you want to pay special attention to, making sure you leave the office on time without taking work home, etc.

When we lack the motivation to do a job, we are overwhelmed by thoughts of TIC (Task Inhibiting Cognitions, i.e. thoughts that inhibit actions). The work seems tedious and useless. This negative energy pushes us to put our work off until later.

To avoid procrastination, you must appeal to TOC thoughts (Task Oriented Cognitions, i.e. thoughts that guide you to action), by looking at the benefits that will come from immediate actions: "If I do it right away, I will be free of it". This state of mind makes them seem less like useless and thankless tasks, making us want to move forward and get our tasks over with, thus engaging more easily in action.

HOW DO I DELEGATE SUCCESSFULLY?

"If you want something done, do it yourself". At least this is what we tend to believe. The result of this thought? Urgent files accumulate on our desks and we perform tasks for which we are sometimes not fully qualified, under the pretext that they are part of our work objectives.

To successfully delegate, you must firstly be aware that nothing can be gained from overloading yourself with work and, secondly, you must trust your team and your colleagues, to whom you can bring expertise during certain tasks, and who can return the favour. A colleague who is more competent at using computers will be able to provide a higher quality of work in the development of web support, while someone who is fluent in written communication will find it easier to answer emails or prepare a meeting report.

Delegating is an option to consider because it saves valuable time and can be a source of good quality work, if we manage to highlight the skills and strengths of each person.

HOW CAN I DISCONNECT FROM WORK ONCE I'VE CLOSED THE OFFICE DOOR?

The growing number of burnout cases proves how vital it is to be able to establish limits. However, in our society, separating work and private life requires a lot of discipline.

Ask yourself this question: How long do you spend working, or thinking or talking about work during weekends and evenings? Are you spending too much time doing this? Do you spend time thinking about the events that happened over the previous week or about the work that awaits you on Monday while trying to enjoy a weekend with your family?

Establishing a boundary is not always possible, nor very easy. These three tips will help you:

- Disconnect as much and as soon as you can from any technology that connects you to your business. Does your boss really need you to answer emails until 9pm?
- Invent a ritual that you practice every day after work that allows you to make the transition from the world of work to your private life. Take a walk, have a cup of coffee on the way home or review your schedule to ensure every-

thing is ready for the next day before leaving;

- Persevere! That little judgmental voice that reminds you that you have not completed a certain task, or warns you that the coming week will be long and arduous, won't go away immediately. Your health and your quality of work are at stake: with no rest or relaxation, you will no longer be able to manage to pay the necessary attention at work, thus risking becoming quickly demotivated or demoralised.

OVER TO YOU

SELF-ANALYSIS

Here is a short list of questions to help you reflect on your time management. Write down your answers on a piece of paper.

- Do you think you manage your time well in your professional life?
  - If yes, what benefits does this bring?
  - If no, what obstacles are you facing?
- Do you have clearly defined professional goals?
- Do you meet the deadlines that have been set?
- Do you feel like you are always working against the clock? Note down some recent examples to demonstrate why you think this.
- Does it seem like you are often distracted or interrupted in your work? If yes, list the distractions.
- Do you manage to properly relax after you have finished your day's work? If not, why? And what are the solutions that might help?

ORGANISATION

> "Objectives and priorities only have meaning if the means of achieving them are prepared and if these means are implemented voluntarily." – Fathi Tlatli

To achieve these goals and manage your priorities, you must provide the means. This organisational tool will help you to make your project happen, and to make it more concrete and measurable from the perspective of your actions and time. First of all, set your goal in simple words, then establish the deadline for its completion (in a year, month or week, depending on the type of goal). List the tasks to do, then evaluate the time needed for each and set deadlines and levels of priority.

This form should be used without moderation, for each new project. By working on planning, you can get a sense of the time needed to achieve your goal and anticipate priority tasks.

WHAT?	HOW?		
Target and important activities in relation to the objectives?	Effectiveness of the method?		
	20/80	I	II
	80/20	III	IV

Priorities and Deadlines © 50MINUTES.com

We want to hear from you!
Leave a comment on your online library
and share your favourite books on social media!

FURTHER READING

BIBLIOGRAPHY

- Bellenger, L. and Couchaere, M. (2004) *Plus efficace et moins stressé. Le bien- être, clé de la performance*. Paris: ESF éditeur.
- Cungi, C. (2006) *Savoir gérer son stress*. Paris: Éditions Retz.
- Fontana, D. (1990) *Gérer le stress*. Liège: Mardaga.
- Gamonnet, F. (1982) *Savoir mieux gérer son temps*. Paris: Éditions d'organisation.
- Geisselhart, R. and Hofmann, C. (2012) *En finir avec le stress*. Brussels: Ixelles éditions.
- Latrobe,D. (2000) *Gérer efficacement son temps et ses priorités. Concilier efficacité et bien- être*. Paris: ESF éditeur.
- Moyson, R. (1998) *Gérer son temps et son stress. Pour un nouvel humanisme*. Brussels: De Boeck Université.
- Testu,F. (1993) *Chronopsychologie et rythmes scolaires*. Paris: Masson.
- Tlatli, F. (2007) *Gérer son temps efficacement. Pour mieux vivre et mieux réussir*. Louvain-la-Neuve: Anthemis.

ADDITIONAL SOURCES

- Online questionnaire to evaluate time management: http://www.rsv.espacedoc.net/fileadmin/forres/ quest-autodiagnostic-gestion-temps.pdf

IMPROVE YOUR GENERAL KNOWLEDGE

IN A BLINK OF AN EYE !

www.50minutes.com